WRITE IT!

W9-CGX-529

WRITE IT!

A Guide
for Research

Third Edition

**Elizabeth Bankhead
Janet Nichols
Dawn Vaughn**

LIBRARIES
UNLIMITED
A Member of the Greenwood Publishing Group
Westport, Connecticut • London

Library of Congress Cataloging-in-Publication Data

Bankhead, Elizabeth.
  Write it! : a guide for research / Elizabeth Bankhead, Janet Nichols,
and Dawn Vaughn.—3rd ed.
      p. cm.
  Includes bibliographical references and index.
  ISBN 978-1-59158-785-9 (alk. paper)
  1. Report writing. 2. Research. I. Nichols, Janet. II. Vaughn, Dawn. III. Title.
  LB1047.3.W75 2009
    808′.02—dc22   2008035925

British Library Cataloguing in Publication Data is available.

Library of Congress Catalog Card Number: 2008035925
ISBN: 978-1-59158-785-9

First published in 2009

Libraries Unlimited, 88 Post Road West, Westport, CT 06881
A Member of the Greenwood Publishing Group, Inc.
www.lu.com

Printed in the United States of America

The paper used in this book complies with the
Permanent Paper Standard issued by the National
Information Standards Organization (Z39.48–1984).

10 9 8 7 6 5 4 3 2 1

Contents

ACKNOWLEDGMENTS

Write It! is designed for students as an easy-to-use guide for citing sources based on the MLA bibliographic format. The idea for publishing such a guide was based on the success of the Cherry Creek High School style manual developed in the 1960s as a joint effort of librarians and teachers to provide a schoolwide standard for bibliographic citations. We acknowledge students and faculty who used that booklet over the years, the teachers and library media specialists who contributed to updates and improvements, and especially the many teachers who continue to maintain high standards in using and citing information.

We acknowledge the excellent learning environment of Cherry Creek High School, where we worked as a team of library media specialists. Cherry Creek High School is representative of the many outstanding schools across the nation where students, teachers, librarians, administrators, and parents work together to encourage excellence in learning and teaching through reading and research. We commend our students for their academic curiosity, persistence, and critical thinking. We thank our administrative team for their leadership in ensuring access to information and technology and our faculty for their commitment to collaborative planning and the integration of information literacy and technology skills into their course assignments.

We hope this third edition of *Write It!* will continue to provide students with a clear, logical process for research. We also pledge to continue to promote collaboratively designed assignments that provide students the opportunity to increase their mastery of both subject content and information literacy and technology skills they will need for success in academics and as citizens. The *Write It! Teacher's Guide* will provide educators with practical resources to integrate standards, thinking skills, and technology into exciting and engaging assignments as well as a planning process that ensures their students receive the support and expertise of both teachers and librarians. The *Write It! Teacher's Guide* can be found at http://www.lu.com/writeit/.

Elizabeth Bankhead, Denver, Colorado
Janet Nichols, Grosse Pointe Farms, Michigan
Dawn Vaughn, Highlands Ranch, Colorado

INTRODUCTION

What Is Research?

Research is a process through which one systematically investigates a subject. Facts, ideas, and expert opinions are gathered, organized, synthesized, and presented. Presentations have traditionally taken the form of a research paper, but increasingly, more presentations are oral or visual using an electronic format. Regardless of format, all good research projects have the following components:

- research begins with a focus question,
- a thesis statement is written in response to the focus question,
- research findings are evaluated and organized for clarity and understanding,
- sources are analyzed, and information is synthesized,
- information is cited, and
- information skills are evaluated for future application.

Research project presentations may take a variety of forms, from a traditional paper or essay to a multimedia presentation. A traditional research paper would include such types of papers as a report, an analytical paper, a cause and effect paper, a comparison and contrast paper, a persuasive essay, an expository essay, or a historical narrative. Some less traditional options reflecting authentic use of information might include a newspaper editorial, a historical journal, a research grant proposal, a photographic essay, a debate, a website, a children's book, a survey, or a podcast.

Regardless of the format of the presentation, the depth of study, or the curricular area of the assignment, the importance of research is that the information is actually used once it is found, organized, and presented. Using the information provides students the opportunity to increase knowledge, to provoke discussion and debate, and to demonstrate critical thinking.

CHAPTER 1

SEARCHING EFFECTIVELY IS SMART!

USING BACKGROUND READING

Research begins by surveying a topic through background reading to provide you with basic information and to allow broadening or narrowing of the subject if necessary. An encyclopedia or textbook is a good starting point to gather general information and keywords that can be used later. While reading, it is a good idea to make a list of names, dates, events, places, descriptive phrases, and synonyms that are relevant to the topic. Names may include people who lived during the time period or those who are involved in the topic. Historical time periods, geographic areas, and specific events are important to note.

UNDERSTANDING KEYWORD STRATEGY

While reading for an overview, it often becomes apparent that the topic is too broad for specific research. Keywords allow you to focus on one aspect of a broad theme, such as global warming. The opposite might be true as well. You might select a very specific topic that, through reading, needs to be broadened to find enough information to support a thesis.

GENERAL TO SPECIFIC

global warming → weather pattern changes caused by global warming

SPECIFIC TO GENERAL

melting glaciers → weather pattern changes caused by global warming

FINDING KEYWORDS

Background reading is essential to the identification of keywords. General encyclopedias and textbooks give overviews of topics that contain basic information, such as people involved, geographic locations, historical time periods, descriptive words, scientific phrases, and synonyms.

People

Names can be used as subjects to locate works about that person or as authors to locate works by that person. Always enter the person's last name first when performing a subject or author search (e.g., *Carson, Rachel*). Enter the person's name in normal order when searching for the name in text (e.g*., Rachel Carson*).

Geographic Locations

Names of places are often used to narrow searches. You might want to confine the search to one continent or country, such as *South America* or *Brazil*. It helps to begin with the specific geographic location and broaden the search until successful results are returned.

Historical Time Periods

Searches can be made more specific by limiting them to a time period, such as the *Middle Ages* or *World War II*, or to a date, such as *1492* or *December 7, 1941.*

Limiting Words

Using words that limit the topic being researched helps to narrow the results. Rather than searching for *global warming*, which would identify an overwhelming amount of information, you might want to add other words or phrases, such as *fossil fuel* or *rain forests*. Also, using words such as *debate, cause, problem,* and *solution* might help to limit the search and give it a focus.

Scientific Phrases

For specific, technical, or scientific information, use the terminology used by the professionals in the field. For example, more specific information will be retrieved using the words *Human Genome Project* rather than searching for *genetics*.

Synonyms

Synonyms are words that have the same meaning as the topic being researched. For example, *teen, teenager, youth, young adult,* and *adolescent* are synonyms. To search for documents containing several synonyms, a keyword search would connect each synonym with the Boolean operator OR and enclose all the synonyms in parentheses. It is important to think of synonyms so they can be used in the advanced search techniques that will be described on pages 7–8.

BROADENING A SEARCH

A graphic method used to describe the different aspects of a broad topic is called webbing. Beginning with the topic in the center, break the topic into several subtopics, then break the subtopics into their parts. By using what's already known along with information from background reading, it is very easy to decide how to approach a topic.

Webbing can be accomplished in an efficient manner either by an individual or by a group of students by using concept-mapping software programs.

WEBBING

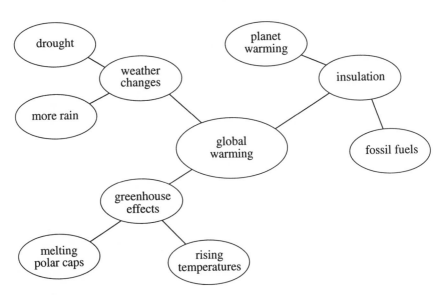

Inspiration Software®, Inc.

USING ADVANCED SEARCH TECHNIQUES

Boolean Operators

In the 1800s, George Boole, an English mathematician, developed a system of algebra, called Boolean algebra, that was used to deal with relationships between mathematical sets. Over the years, researchers have developed keyword searches using words in the same way Boole dealt with relationships between mathematical sets. There are three basic Boolean operators used in keyword searching to combine or eliminate terms: AND, OR, and NOT. Notice that the Boolean operators are typed in all capital letters. Although this is not always required, it is good practice to type them in all capital letters because some databases and search engines require upper case.

AND

This Boolean operator is used to narrow the keyword search by combining terms. All the terms must be included in the results. Some databases or search engines use the plus (+) symbol instead of the Boolean operator AND.

Examples:	castles AND europe
	castles + europe
Results:	information must contain both of the words
	castles and *Europe*

OR

This Boolean operator is used to develop a broad search for information on any of the words used in the keyword search statement.

Example:	teenager OR adolescent
Result:	information contains either one of the words
	teenager or *adolescent*

NOT

This Boolean operator is used when a term is to be excluded from the results of a keyword search. Some databases and search engines use the minus (−) symbol instead of the Boolean operator NOT.

Examples:	microwave NOT recipe
	microwave −recipe
Results:	information contains the term *microwave* but excludes any information that includes the word *recipe*

Proximity Operators

In addition to the three Boolean operators, there are several proximity operators. These operators, ADJ and NEAR, help create a relationship between words by requiring that the search terms occur next to each other or close together in a document.

ADJ (adjacent)

When two words are connected by ADJ, the terms must appear adjacent to each other in the order entered. Some databases or search engines place quotation marks around the phrase in place of the proximity operator ADJ.

Examples:	global ADJ warming
	"global warming"
Results:	information that contains the terms *global* and *warming* together and only in that order

NEAR

When NEAR is used between two words, a more complex search can be achieved than with the operator AND. NEAR requires that the two words appear close together in the document and in any order. This search will result in a relationship between *medieval* and *castles*, regardless of the order in which they appear in the document.

Example:	medieval NEAR castles
Result:	information with the words *medieval* and *castles* near each other and in any order

Other Search Operators

Truncation/Wild Card

Truncation, which may also be called *wild card*, is a powerful strategy to use in keyword searching. This technique is particularly helpful when there are many variations of the same word that would be useful in search results. By leaving off the end of the word, all forms of the word will be included in the search. As a signal to the computer that truncation is being used, letters will be replaced with symbols such as an asterisk (*), question mark (?), or pound sign (#), depending on the search engine. Some search engines also allow you to replace a letter inside a word with a wild card.

Examples:	forest*
	wom*n
Results:	information containing any one of the words *forest*, *forests*, *forester*, *forestation*, and *foresting*
	information containing either the word *woman* or *women*

LIMITING

Limiting your results can be very helpful when evaluating a lot of information. Most search engines allow you to limit your results in many different ways. Check the advanced searching link or the help screen to see what limiters a site allows. Common limiters that are very helpful are number of results, date of publication, language, type of material (map, video, images), computer file format, and domain name of websites.

Examples:	number of articles: 50
	language: French
	date range: past year
Results:	only the first 50 articles that meet the search criteria will be listed
	all information will be in *French*
	information will be limited to articles published over the last 12 months

NATURAL LANGUAGE SEARCHING

Natural language searching allows you to ask a question and the computer to automatically construct the search. Supplying keywords is not necessary. This method of searching is especially helpful for the beginning researcher. Natural language searching is not available in all databases, so be sure to check the help screens in the database you are using.

Example:	What is the greenhouse effect on tropical rain forests?
Results:	information that contains both the phrases *greenhouse effect* and *tropical rain forests*

COMBINING OPERATORS FOR MORE ADVANCED SEARCHES

In searching libraries and scholarly databases, it can be helpful to design an advanced search. Parentheses are used to group terms that are searched first, and then the results within the parentheses are searched using Boolean operators. This grouping of terms is called "nesting" and must be used for terms that are linked by OR within a larger search. It is usually better to use simple searches on Internet websites since the traditional operators may not be used by a particular search engine.

Example:	"greenhouse effect" AND tropical AND ("rain forest*" OR rainforest*) NOT "south america"
Result:	information containing any one of the words *rain forest*, *rain forests*, *rainforest*, or *rainforests*, combined with the words *tropical* and *greenhouse effect*, but no articles that include information about *South America*

Example:	(teen* OR youth OR adolescent OR "young adult") AND "drug abuse"
Result:	information containing any one of the words *teen*, *teens*, *teenage*, *teenager*, *teenagers*, *youth*, *adolescent*, *adolescents*, or *young adult*, combined with the phrase *drug abuse*

Example:	("middle age*" OR medieval) NEAR castle* AND europe AND NOT (travel OR tour*)
Results:	information containing any one of the terms *middle age*, *middle ages*, or *medieval* if they are located near the words *castle* or *castles*, if the information also contains the term *Europe* but the information will not contain any of the terms *travel*, *tour*, *tours*, *touring*, *tourist*, or *tourists*

SUMMARY OF OPERATORS

AND — Boolean operator locates all information containing both of the terms in the same document. A plus sign (+) may be used instead of AND in some instances.

OR — Boolean operator locates all information containing either word but not necessarily both words in the same document.

NOT — Boolean operator eliminates any information with that term. Some search engines require using AND with NOT (AND NOT), or a minus sign (−) instead of NOT in some instances.

ADJ — Words must occur together and in that order.

NEAR — Words must occur within a specified number of words but in any order.

* — When an asterisk is used as truncation (at the end of a word), any form of the word before the asterisk will be returned. When the symbol is used as a wild card by replacing a character in a word, information will be returned with any letter in place of the wild card.

" " — Words inside quotation marks will be searched together and in that order.

( ) — Words inside parentheses will be searched first, and then the results of that preliminary search are linked with terms outside the parentheses.

SUMMARY: CONSTRUCTING KEYWORD SEARCHES

There is no one way to construct keyword searches. Each database and search engine may use operators and symbols in a unique way. Once you understand the power of keyword searching, you can easily apply it to different sites using their system. Help pages are a great place to start when first using a database or search engine. Select the help option on the main screen. By taking time to look at specific search features of a database, frustration can be eliminated and time saved.

CHAPTER 2

BEING SELECTIVE AND FOCUSED IS IMPORTANT!

FINDING INFORMATION

Determining the best place to begin to look for information is one of the first steps in successful research. After selecting a topic, ask the following questions:

1. *What do I know about my topic?*

Start a list of facts and terms.

2. *Where can I find a definition, an overview, or general information about my topic?*

Begin with reading in an encyclopedia, textbook, or general magazine article. This will help you develop your thesis statement, identify keywords, and plan your research.

3. *Now that I have background information about my topic, what sources should I use?*

Ask the following questions:

- *Is my topic current?* If so, magazines, newspapers, and the Internet will be useful sources. If you use books, you will need to pay attention to the copyright date.

- *Is my topic historical?* If so, you will want to use reference books as well as specific books on your subject. Although you may find some good information in magazine articles and on the Internet, you will not want to start with or rely only on those sources. The copyright date of the books chosen is not as important as the content.

- *How much time do I have to complete my research?* If you have only a short time to complete your research, consider what you can realistically accomplish. Limit your resources to those you will realistically use.

- *Are certain types of sources required by the assignment? If so, what are they?* List specific requirements and be sure to locate each type of source or the specific number of sources required. For suggestions of good sources to meet requirements, use the section called "Meeting Special Requirements" on pages 15–17.

EVALUATING INFORMATION

Basic Evaluation Questions

An important part of research that is often ignored is the evaluation of information found during the research process. Regardless of where the information is found, use these questions to decide its value.

1. *Who is the author?*

   Is the author an authority on the subject?

   What are the author's credentials?

   What is the author's affiliation?

2. *Is the material presented accurately?*

   Can the information be verified by other sources?

   Are the facts consistent?

   Is the information backed up by facts, or are conclusions drawn from opinions?

   Is there a bibliography or other reference points?

3. *Is the information current?*

   When was the last update written?

   Does the information concur with the latest research on the subject?

4. *Is the information biased?*

   Who published the material?

   Is the publisher affiliated with a biased organization?

   Does the material present only one side of an issue?

   What is the purpose of the publication?

Internet Evaluation Questions

When using Internet sites for research, additional questions must be asked.

1. *What is the domain of the Web page?*

   Can the domain name be used to verify the information presented on a Web page?

   Does the domain name indicate potential bias?

   ### Common Domain Names

.biz	=	business site
.com	=	commercial site
.gov	=	government site
.info	=	informative site
.int	=	international treaty–based organization site
.name	=	real names, nicknames, screen names, pseudonyms
.org	=	organization site, usually nonprofit
.edu	=	university site
.mil	=	military site
.net	=	networked service provider

2. *For whom is the information intended?*

   Although the information may be accurate, would a website developed by an elementary school class be a good source of information for a research paper?

   If a website is maintained by an organization with a definite point of view (e.g., Greenpeace or the National Rifle Association), should the information from that site be verified in other sources or sites?

3. *Is the author listed?*

   Can the author be contacted?

   Even if a specific author is connected with an educational site, should the information be verified in other sources or sites?

DEVELOPING THE THESIS STATEMENT

Good research begins with a focus question. The thesis statement should be a clear, concise answer to that focus question.

Focus Question: Why are scientists concerned about global warming?

Thesis Statement: Global warming is causing a change in the earth's weather patterns that will have disastrous effects.

Focus Question: What effect did the Crusades have on Europe?

Thesis Statement: The Crusades directly contributed to the rising influence of the Catholic Church in Europe.

Focus Question: Can the novels *Huckleberry Finn* and *Catcher in the Rye* be compared?

Thesis Statement: The novels *Huckleberry Finn* and *Catcher in the Rye* have main characters who experience a rite of passage from adolescence to adulthood.

What a Thesis Statement Is Not

1. A topic by itself cannot serve as a thesis statement.

   Not a Thesis Statement: This paper will discuss the concerns scientists have about global warming.

2. A question cannot serve as a thesis statement. The thesis statement is developed from a question.

   Not a Thesis Statement: What problems are associated with global warming?

3. A general statement without a point of view cannot serve as a thesis statement.

   Not a Thesis Statement: Much has been written about global warming.

What a Thesis Statement Is

1. A complete sentence summarizing the point of view in your paper.

2. A specific statement of the main idea.

3. A statement reflecting the position taken in your paper.

MEETING SPECIAL REQUIREMENTS

Sometimes a research assignment requires that specific types of information be included. The required types of information often fall into broad subject areas, such as art or literature, or basic categories, such as statistics or maps. The following are some examples of standard sources found in most libraries or directly available on the Internet that would provide a good starting point for meeting special requirements.

Art

Artcyclopedia: The Guide to Great Art on the Internet. Ed. John Malyon. 2007. 20 Apr. 2008 <http://www.artcyclopedia.com>.

Gardner, Helen. Gardner's Art through the Ages. 12th ed. Belmont: Thomson, 2005.

Grove Art Online. 2008. Oxford UP. 20 Apr. 2008 <http://www. groveart.com>.

Biography

Biography.com. 1996–2007. A & E Television Networks. 20 Apr. 2008 <http://www.biography.com>.

Current Biography. New York: Wilson, 1940–.

Garrity, John Arthur, ed. American National Biography. New York: Oxford UP, 1999.

Global Issues

CountryReports.org. 20 Apr. 2008 <http://www.countryreports. org/>.

Global Perspectives on the United States: A Nation by Nation Survey. 3 vols. Great Barrington: Berkshire, 2007.

World Geography: Understanding a Changing World. 2008. ABC-CLIO. 20 Apr. 2008 <http://www.worldgeography. abc-clio.com/Home/Default.aspx>.

History

Dictionary of American History. 3rd ed. 10 vols. New York: Scribner's, 2003.

American Memory. 21 Apr. 2008. Lib. of Congress, Washington. 30 Apr. 2008 <http://memory.loc.gov/ammem/index.html>.

United States at War. 2008. ABC-CLIO. 20 Apr. 2008 <http://www.usatwar.abc-clio.com/Home/Default.aspx>.

Literature

Contemporary Literary Criticism. 171 vols. to date. Farmington Hills: Thomson, 1973–.

Litfinder for Schools. 2008. Thomson. Cherry Creek High School Lib., Greenwood Village, CO. 29 Apr. 2008 <http://www.litfinder.com/home.asp>.

Poets.org. 1997–2008. Academy of American Poets. 20 Apr. 2008 <http://www.poets.org/>.

Maps

Hammond World Atlas Corporation. The World Almanac 2008 World Atlas. 2nd ed. Union: Hammond, 2008.

Konstam, Angus. Historical Atlas of Ancient Greece. New York: Mercury Books, 2006.

Maps 101: The Educational Resource Online. 2008. Maps.com. 20 Apr. 2008 <http://www.maps101.com/Application/Index.aspx>.

Medicine

Diseases and Disorders. New York: Marshall Cavendish, 2008.

Health Source—Consumer Edition. 2008. EBSCO. Cherry Creek High School Lib. Greenwood Village, CO. 20 Apr. 2008 <http://web.ebscohost.com>.

National Institutes of Health. 18 Apr. 2007. United States Dept. of Health and Human Services. 20 Apr. 2008 <http://www.nih.gov/>.

Primary Sources

Unger, Irwin, ed. American Issues: A Primary Source Reader in United States History. Englewood Cliffs: Prentice Hall, 1994.

American Memory. 21 Apr. 2008. Lib. of Congress, Washington. 1 May 2008 <http://emory.loc.gov/ammem/index.html>.

Pro/Con

Introducing Issues with Opposing Viewpoints. 49 vols. to date. Detroit: Greenhaven, 2006–.

Issues and Controversies. 2008. Facts on File. Cherry Creek High
    School Lib., Greenwood Village, CO. 20 Apr. 2008 <http://
    www.2facts.com/>.

Opposing Viewpoints Resource Center. 2008. Gale. Cherry Creek
    High School Lib., Greenwood Village, CO. 20 Apr. 2008
    <http://find.galegroup.com/>.

Science

Nature.com. 2008. Nature Publishing Group. 20 Apr. 2008
    <http://www.nature.com/index.html>.

Science Resource Center. 2008. Gale. Cherry Creek High School
    Lib., Greenwood Village, CO. 20 Apr. 2008 <http://galenet.
    galegroup.com>.

Van Nostrand's Scientific Encyclopedia. 10th ed. New York: Wiley,
    2008.

Statistics

World News Digest. 2008. Facts on File. Cherry Creek High
    School Lib., Greenwood Village, CO. 20 Apr. 2008 <http://
    www.2facts.com/>.

FedStats. 2007. United States Govt. 20 Apr. 2008 <http://www.
    fedstats.gov/>.

United States Bureau of the Census. Statistical Abstract of the
    United States: 2008. Washington: GPO, 2007.

World Almanac and Book of Facts: 2008. New York: World
    Almanac Books, 2008.

CHAPTER 3

STAYING ORGANIZED SAVES TIME!

USING RESEARCH LOGS

It is important to keep track of sources used and information located during research. Bibliography and note cards are traditional ways of doing this. However, with the tremendous amount of information available electronically, it is also important to keep track of the path followed as you begin searching for information. One way to do this is to keep a research log. A research log is simply a record of the specific path followed in finding information.

There is no standard format for a research log. The format a researcher chooses to use is entirely up to personal preference and has to be one that makes sense for the type of project and the types of sources being used. The sites searched, along with the keywords used to access information and locate books, should be listed. In this way, specific sites and books can be easily found again, and time can be saved by not repeating the search. Printed copies of information and online catalog records can be attached to a research log with important details highlighted.

If you choose to e-mail useful articles to yourself, create an e-mail box for all articles related to your topic (e.g., global warming) and write brief notes regarding the content of the articles. Similarly, as you bookmark websites to use in your research, create a separate folder for your topic (e.g., global warming).

SAMPLE RESEARCH LOGS

BIOLOGY RESEARCH LOG: RESEARCH PAPER

Topic: Global warming—what is the problem, what solutions are suggested

Keywords: *Limiting keywords:*
  global warming   *problem*
  greenhouse effect   *solution*
  ozone layer   *cause*
  climate change   *effect*
  greenhouse gases   *debate*
  carbon footprint   *controversy*
  polar ice caps
  Earth Day

Databases:
  SIRS Researcher
  Subject Search   *global warming*
  Keyword Search   *"global warming" AND*
                                         controversy AND debate

  Opposing Viewpoints   *global warming*
  Facts.com   *global warming*
  Today's Science   *climate change (listed under*
                                         "hot topics")

Online Catalog:
  keyword   *global warming*
  keyword   *atmosphere AND temperature*
  keyword   *greenhouse effect*
  subject   *global warming*

The Internet:
  Google   *"global warming"*
                                        +"climate change"
  Yahoo   *"global warming"*
                                        "climate change"

SPANISH RESEARCH LOG

Topic: *The culture of Mexico*

Keywords:

> *Mexico*   *Cinco de Mayo*
> *culture*   *mariachis*
> *marriage*   *Catholicism*
> *family*   *bull fighting*
> *arts*
> *music*
> *education*
> *food*
> *religion*
> *mores*

Online Catalog:

> *Keyword:*   *mexico AND culture*
> *Subject:*   *Mexico—Social Life and customs*

Web:

> *Google*   *"culture of mexico"*
> *Culturgrams*   *Mexico*

PREPARING BIBLIOGRAPHY CARDS

When using bibliography cards, each source used is cited on a separate card. Bibliography cards make it easy to alphabetize sources when preparing the Works Cited or Bibliography page.

A different approach is to use computer printouts from online catalogs and other databases as a substitute for bibliography cards. However, all the necessary information for a citation must be included on the printout. Remember, the purpose of preparing bibliography cards or keeping computer printouts is to make the task of preparing a Works Cited or Bibliography page as easy as possible.

Use the sample citations that appear in the next chapter as a guide for citing specific kinds of sources.

Examples of Bibliography Cards

Book

> Lynas, Mark. _Six Degrees: Our Future on a Hotter_
> _Planet_. Washington: National Geographic,
> 2008.

Magazine

> Wagner, Cynthia G. ''Climate Change and Global
> Conflicts.'' _The Futurist_ Mar.-Apr. 2008: 1.
> WilsonSelect Plus. FirstSearch. Wayne State
> University Lib. 24 Apr. 2008 <http://www.
> firstsearch.com>.

TAKING NOTES

Note cards contain supporting information such as facts, statistics, direct quotations, definitions, or opinions of authorities, all of which will be cited within the paper. Only one idea should be written on each note card. That way, the cards can be rearranged in any order during the planning stages of the paper. There is no need to include the complete bibliographic citation on the note card, only the first part of the citation.

There are many different methods of note taking. Using note cards as in the following examples is the more traditional method. As an alternative, you may want to collect your notes through an online source that links your notes to the online bibliography or use the printouts of your articles to highlight important passages. If you choose to collect your notes in a word processing document rather than on cards, be sure to label each note just as you would on a note card. Anytime you cut and paste text from a source, label the note as a *direct quote*. When entering notes that you have paraphrased or summarized, label the note appropriately. Regardless of the method you use for note taking, careful organization of your notes as well as citing the sources you use are research management tools that will help you when you begin writing your paper.

Types of Note Cards

Direct Quotation Note

Temperature changes {topic heading for easy
    sorting}
Hansen

''The greatest threat of climate change for
    human beings lies in the potential
    destabilization of the massive ice sheets in
    Greenland and Antarctica.''

1 {page number where quotation appears}

Paraphrased Note

> *Temperature changes*
>
> *Hansen*
>
> *The most serious consequence of rising global temperatures is a change in the polar ice caps in Greenland and Antarctica.*
>
> 1

Summarized Note

> *Temperature changes*
>
> *Hansen*
>
> *Melting of polar ice caps most serious effect*
>
> 1

OUTLINING A PRESENTATION

One way to organize information for presentation is to develop an outline. An outline will provide a framework for using information to form logical paragraphs that support a thesis statement. An outline can also be extremely useful in creating a visual presentation. When using the outline as points in a visual presentation, change the numbering system to a system of bullets or other visual cues.

Steps to Developing an Outline

1. Sort notes by topic headings.

2. Organize topics so that there is a logical development.

3. Create subtopics that are logical divisions of the main topic. Each "A" must have a "B" and each "1" must have a "2" because concepts cannot logically be divided into only one part.

4. Make sure that the wording of each line is consistent in form and phrasing. Outlines may be either phrases or sentences, depending on the teacher's requirements.

SAMPLE OUTLINE

GLOBAL WARMING

I. Problem

   A. Changes in weather

   B. Causes

   C. Environmental disaster

II. Weather changes

   A. Predictions

      1. Study the past

      2. Develop models

   B. Patterns

      1. History

      2. Models—future

         a. Depletion of resources

         b. Food production

         c. Water supply

         d. Health

         e. Ecosystem

III. Solutions

   A. Alter reliance on fossil fuels

   B. Time line

   C. Nations reach agreements

   D. Lifestyle changes

SAMPLE PAPER

There is no specific requirement for the formatting of a title page for a research paper. What follows is an example only. Notice that the paper is double spaced throughout with indented first lines at the beginning of each new paragraph. The sample paper provides a possible example to follow, but always check with your instructor as to specific requirements for your assignment. These may include title page, spacing requirements, page numbering, and Works Cited or Bibliography page. As you proofread your paper, always double-check any formatting requirements of your assignment.

Global Warming, Global Warning

Sara Castillo

Biology
Mr. Brooks
May 24, 2008

Castillo 1

Global warming is causing a change in the earth's weather patterns that will have disastrous effects. ''Increasing human populations, rising affluence, and continued dependence on energy derived from fossil fuels are at the crux of the issue'' (Johnson 2). Unless this issue is resolved and solutions are found, an environmental disaster will occur.

Scientists have studied past weather patterns and developed models to predict the future. According to Lynas (49) these models suggest we have not yet reached the critical tipping point, but it may not be far away. Scientists' expectations for climate change are supported by evidence gathered from around the world (Dow and Downing 20–21). The potential for major changes in the polar ice sheets in Greenland and Antarctica will cause an irreversible disaster (Hansen 1). As our climate warms scientists warn that the ''depletion of resources on which livelihoods are based is the most critical effect of such change'' (Wagner 1). Climate change will affect food production, water supplies, health, and ecosystems (Dow and Downing 54–61).

What is the cause of global warming? The use of fossil fuels for the past two centuries is generally accepted as the major cause of global warming (Johnson 1). Lynas (281) concludes that we have only seven years before facing the danger of uncontrollable global warming. Nations struggle with reaching any universal agreement on how to reduce reliance on fossil fuels. In the meantime individuals can make a commitment to life style changes to reduce the greenhouse gases emitted as a result of the way we live (Dow and Downing 89).

Castillo 2

WORKS CITED

Dow, Kirstin, and Thomas E. Downing. <u>The Atlas of Climate Change</u>. Berkeley: U of California P, 2006.

Hansen, Jim. ''The Effect on Animals.'' Debra Miller. ''The World's Most Serious Environmental Problem Is Global Warming.'' <u>Opposing Viewpoints Resource Center</u>. Gale. Wayne State U Lib. 24 Apr. 2008 <http://Galegroup.com>.

Johnson, Bruce E. <u>The Global Warming Desk Reference</u>. Westport: Greenwood, 2002. NetLibrary. Wayne State U Lib. 21 Apr. 2008 <http://www.netlibrary.com>.

Lynas, Mark. <u>Six Degrees: Our Future on a Hotter Planet</u>. Washington: National Geographic, 2008.

Wagner, Cynthia G. ''Climate Change and Global Conflicts.'' <u>The Futurist</u> Mar.–Apr. 2008: 1. WilsonSelect Plus. FirstSearch. Wayne State U Lib. 24 Apr. 2008 <http://www.firstsearch.com>.

CHAPTER 4

CITING SOURCES IS REQUIRED!

ACADEMIC EXPECTATIONS

Before you begin to research, you need to have a clear under-standing of your instructor's requirements for the type of research project, the source requirements, and the time line for completion. In addition, there are *__universal requirements for academic research__* regardless of the instructor, school, or purpose of the research.

Researchers rely on a body of previous knowledge to investigate, examine, and argue their ideas. *Academic ethics* requires that when-ever a researcher uses the words or ideas of another, the researcher must cite the original source. This is done for two reasons:

Others reading your work may find that they would like to look at the original source for certain facts or ideas. By pro-viding complete citations for those sources, this is possible. Much good research is done by following the path other researchers have begun.

When you use the words or ideas of another researcher, you *must* give credit to that researcher. It is never appropriate or ethical to present another researcher's work as your own. A simple rule to follow is "give credit where credit is due." To do otherwise is academically unethical and brings with it se-rious consequences. The term for presenting another's work as your own is *plagiarism*.

PLAGIARISM

Plagiarism is use of another person's work or ideas without acknowledging the author, whether the work is published or unpublished, professional or amateur, or graphic or digital. The most flagrant example of plagiarism is turning in a complete paper or project that is the work of another. More often, plagiarism occurs when a writer uses parts of another's work without crediting the source. This can be done by simply cutting and pasting the author's words or by paraphrasing the words and ideas of the author. In either case, when another's words, phrases, ideas, opinions, designs, or facts are used, credit must be given. When words and ideas are noted, the source should be clearly indicated on the note card to help you differentiate your own thoughts from others that *must* be cited.

Because plagiarism is actually theft of intellectual property, it is considered a serious offense. In the corporate world such thefts are prosecuted, in the publishing world plagiarism can damage or end a career, and in the academic world it can result in the loss of a grade, dismissal from class, or even more serious penalties. Schools, colleges, and universities take plagiarism very seriously and will have a written policy that outlines the consequences of plagiarizing another's work. Simply stated, do not ever submit someone else's work as your own whether an entire project or even one idea or quotation.

A good way to understand plagiarism is to identify with someone who owns intellectual property. Imagine a situation where you have written a story, poem, song lyrics, or computer program and someone else claims it as their work by using it without asking permission or by selling it for profit. You would feel you deserved credit and compensation if the idea had been sold.

IMPORTANT NOTE

It does not matter whether using another's work is intentional or unintentional. If you do so without crediting the source, you are committing plagiarism.

PARENTHETICAL DOCUMENTATION EXAMPLES

Avoid interrupting the flow of writing by placing the parenthetical note at the first natural pause in the sentence. The parenthetical reference comes before the punctuation mark that ends the sentence, clause, or phrase containing the quoted or paraphrased material. An exception is when the quotation is longer than four lines; in this case, set it off from the text by beginning a new line, indenting one inch from the left margin and double-spacing, without adding quotation marks.

Author Name Used in the Text

If the author's name is stated in the text of the paper, include only the page number of the work in the parenthetical reference. There is no need to repeat the author's name in the parentheses.

> According to Mandell, "modern sports, therefore, are a particular adaption to modern economic, social, and political life ..." (3).

Authors with the Same Last Name

If citing works by authors with the same last name, the first initial of the author's first name must be included in the parenthetical reference.

> "Main Street is the climax of civilization" (S. Lewis 6).

More Than One Source by the Same Author

If citing more than one work by an author, include the author's last name (if it does not appear in the text of your paper), a shortened form of the title, and the page on which the information appears.

> "My infatuation with the study of animate nature grew rapidly into a full-fledged love affair" (Mowat, Never Cry 3).

> Dian Fossey reflected, "I had a deep wish to see and live with wild animals in a world that hadn't yet been completely changed by humans" (Mowat, Woman 1).

No Page Numbers in Source

If the source you are citing has no page numbers or any other kind of numbering, no page number can be given in the parenthetical reference.

> "... glaciers are warning us of the buildup of dangerous gases" (Nash).

SAMPLE CITATIONS

Sources used in research are documented in two ways. First, a parenthetical note acknowledges the source of information within the text of the paper. Second, a complete citation is listed on the final page of a research paper in alphabetical order under the title *Works Cited* or *Bibliography*. *Works Cited* lists only those sources actually used and cited in the paper. A *Bibliography* page takes the place of a *Works Cited* page because it is a complete list of all sources examined, whether or not the source was actually cited. Individual assignments will specify whether to use a *Works Cited* or a *Bibliography* page.

For each type of source listed on the following pages, the parenthetical citation is shown first in parentheses as it would appear in the text. The full bibliographic citation it refers to follows as it would appear in a *Bibliography* or *Works Cited* page.

You will not find an example to fit every citation circumstance. The important point to remember about citing sources is to be **consistent**. Use only one citation style, double-check your style manual for each citation instead of relying on your memory to cite sources correctly, and when in doubt, check with a librarian or your instructor for guidance.

QUICK GUIDE TO CITATIONS

Number refers you to page where citation can be found.

Books

One Author

(Lynas 281)

Lynas, Mark. <u>Six Degrees: Our Future on a Hotter Planet</u>.
Washington: National Geographic, 2008.

Two or Three Authors

(Dow and Downing 21)

Dow, Kirstin, and Thomas E. Downing. <u>The Atlas of Climate
Change</u>. Berkeley: U of California P, 2006.

More Than Three Authors

(Hillman 24)

Hillman, Mayer, et al. <u>The Suicidal Planet: How to Prevent
Global Climate Catastrophe</u>. New York: St. Martin's, 2007.

No Author

(<u>American Heritage</u> 268)

<u>American Heritage Science Dictionary</u>. Boston: Houghton, 2005.

Editor

(Wood 275)

Wood, Richard A., ed. <u>The Weather Almanac</u>. Detroit: Gale, 2004.

Corporate Author

(American Medical Association 268)

American Medical Association. <u>The American Medical
Association Concise Encyclopedia of Medicine</u>. Ed. Martin
S. Lipsky. New York: Random, 2006.

Work in an Anthology

(Poe 210)

Poe, Edgar Allan. "The Raven." Hazel Felleman. <u>The Best
Loved Poems of the American People</u>. New York:
Doubleday, 1936. 209–211.

Multivolume Work with an Editor

(Considine 2295)

Considine, Glenn D., ed. Van Nostrand's Scientific Encyclopedia. Vol. 2. Hoboken: Wiley, 2008.

Multivolume Work with an Author and Editor

(Thurman 180)

Thurman, Robert A. F. "Buddhism." Encyclopedia of Asian History. Ed. Ainslie T. Embree. Vol. 1. New York: Scribner's, 1988.

Multivolume Work with a Different Title for Each Volume

(Ecology 57)

Ecology and Environment: The Cycles of Life. New York: Oxford UP, 2003. Vol. 6 of The New Encyclopedia of Science. 9 vols.

Excerpts from Criticism Cited in a Single Work

(Quinn 430)

Quinn, Arthur Hobson. Edgar Allan Poe: A Critical Biography. Rpt. in Poetry Criticism. Vol. 1 Ed. Robyn V. Young. Detroit: Gale, 1991. 430.

Government Publication

(U.S. Census Bureau 421)

United States Census Bureau. Statistical Abstract of the United States: 2007. Washington: GPO, 2006.

Almanac

("Some Notable" 243)

"Some Notable New Books, 2005." The World Almanac and Book of Facts 2007. New York: World Almanac, 2007.

("America's Ten")

"America's Ten Most Endangered Rivers, 2007." Infoplease. 2007. Pearson. 29 Apr. 2008 <http://www.infoplease.com/science/environment/americas-endangered-rivers-2007.html>.

Pamphlet

(<u>Funding</u> 9)

<u>Funding Education Beyond High School: The Guide to Federal Student Aid</u>. Washington: GPO, 2007.

E-Book

(Johnson 2)

Johnson, Bruce E. <u>The Global Warming Desk Reference</u>. Westport: Greenwood, 2002. NetLibrary. Wayne State U Lib. 21 Apr. 2008 <http://www.netlibrary.com>.

(Cooper 121)

Cooper, James Fenimore. <u>The Deerslayer</u> [Etext-No. 3285] Project Gutenberg. 2002. 24 Apr. 2008 <http://www.gutenberg. org/etext/3285>.

(Carlson)

Carlson, Eric W. "Edgar Allan Poe." <u>Dictionary of Literary Biography: American Short-Story Writers before 1880</u>. Ed. Bobby Ellen Kimbel. Vol. 74 of <u>Dictionary of Literary Biography</u>. Detroit: Gale, 1988. Gale Literary Databases. Wayne State U Lib. Apr. 24 2008 <http://galenet.galegroup. com>.

Encyclopedias

Article from a General Encyclopedia with an Author

(Wertheim 224)

Wertheim, Albert. "Globe Theatre." <u>The World Book Encyclopedia</u>. 2004 ed.

Article from a General Encyclopedia without an Author

("Ballooning" 117)

"Ballooning." <u>Encyclopedia Americana</u>. 2001 ed.

Article from a Specialized Encyclopedia

(McKay 485)

McKay, Alex. "Tibet." <u>Encyclopedia of Modern Asia</u>. Ed. David Levinson and Karen Christensen. 2002 ed. Vol. 5. New York: Thomson, 2002. 484–486.

Article from a General Online Encyclopedia

("Globe Theater")

"Globe Theater." <u>Wikipedia</u>. 21 May 2008. Wikipedia Foundation,
   Inc. 24 Apr. 2008 <http://en.wikipedia.org/wiki/Globe_Theater>.

Article from a Specialized Online Encyclopedia

("Asian and Near Eastern Art")

"Asian and Near Eastern Art." <u>Encyclopedia Smithsonian</u>.
   21 Apr. 2008 <http://www.si.edu/Encyclopedia_SI/
   Art_and_Design?AsianArt.htm>.

Magazines

Article with an Author

(Gugliotta 42)

Gugliotta, Guy. "Rare Breed." <u>Smithsonian</u> Mar. 2008: 38–47.

Article from a Subscription Database That Produces Its Own Information

(Clemmitt)

Clemmitt, Marcia. "Preventing Memory Loss." <u>CQ Researcher</u>
   4 Apr. 2008: 289–312. 27 Apr. 2008 <http://library.cqpress.
   com/cqresearcher/cqresrre2008040400>.

Article from a Subscription Database That Collects Information from a Variety of Sources

(Nash)

Nash, Madeleine J. "Chronicling the Ice." <u>Smithsonian</u> July
   2007: 66–74. <u>MAS Ultra School Edition</u>. EBSCO. Cherry
   Creek High School Lib., Greenwood Village, CO. 24 Apr.
   2008 <http://search.ebscohost.com>.

Article from the Internet with an Author

(Gandel)

Gandel, Cathie. "Bamboo Steps Up." <u>Smithsonian.com</u> 21
   Mar. 2008. 24 Apr. 2008 <http://www.smithsonianmag.com/
   science-nature/bamboo.html?c=y&page=2>.

Article from the Internet without an Author

("Medical Miracles")

"Medical Miracles Slipping Away as Extinction Claims Species." Environment News Service 23 Apr. 2008. 24 Apr. 2008 <http://www.ens-newswire.com/ens/apr2008/2008-04-23-01.asp>.

Newspapers

Article with an Author

(Pasternak 7A)

Pasternak, Judy. "EPA Workers Report Political Pressure." Denver Post 24 Apr. 2008: 7A.

Article from a Subscription Database

(Fleming)

Fleming, Sam. "UN Issues Alert Over Soaring Food Prices." Daily Mail [United Kingdom] 12 Apr. 2008. Newspaper Source. EBSCO. Cherry Creek High School Lib., Greenwood Village, CO. 27 Apr. 2008 <http://search.ebscohost.com/login.aspx?direct=true&db=nfh&AN=2W62W63660084786&site=ehost-live>.

Article from an Online Newspaper

(Bodeen)

Bodeen, Christopher. "100,000-Strong Force to Protect Olympics." Washington Post 19 June 2008. 20 June 2008 <www.washingtonpost.com>.

Editorial

("Cell Phone")

"Cell Phone Rights." Editorial. Rocky Mountain News 28 Apr. 2008: News 30.

("Global Warming")

"Global Warming and Your Wallet." Editorial. New York Times 6 July 2007: 14. Newspaper Source. EBSCO. Cherry Creek High School Lib., Greenwood Village, CO. 29 Apr. 2008 <http://web.ebscohost.com/>.

Specialized Sources

Art/Photographs

(Bierstadt)

Bierstadt, Albert. <u>Rocky Pool, New Hampshire</u>. Denver
Art Museum, Denver.

(da Vinci)

da Vinci, Leonardo. <u>Mona Lisa</u>. 1503–1506. Louvre, Paris. 30
Apr. 2008 <http://www.louvre.fr/llv/oeuvres/detail_notice.jsp>.

Article in a Corporate Website

("Learn About Cancer")

"Learn About Cancer." <u>Cancer.org</u>. 2008. American Cancer
Society. 22 Apr. 2008 <http://www.cancer.org>.

Blog

(Anderson)

Anderson, Brett. "Arctic Haze, a New Culprit to Warming."
Weblog entry. 28 Apr. 2008. Global Warming Blog.
<u>Accuweather.com</u>. 28 Apr. 2008 <http://global-warming.
accuweather.com/2008/04/arctic_haze_a_new_culprit_to_
w.html>.

Cartoon

(White A27)

White, Grady. Cartoon. <u>New York Times</u> 28 Apr. 2008: A27.

(Toles)

Toles, Tom. Cartoon. <u>washingtonpost.com</u> 28 Apr. 2008. 30
Apr. 2008 <http://www.washingtonpost.com/wp-srv/opinions/
cartoonsandvideos/toles_main.html>.

Corporate Website

(ESPN)

ESPN: The World Leader in Sports. 2008. <u>ESPN Internet
Ventures</u>. 23 Apr. 2008 <http://espn.go.com/>.

E-Mail Communication

(Anderson)

Anderson, Brett. "Re: Arctic Haze." E-mail to Lori Chen. 30
Apr. 2008.

Interview

(Bush)

Bush, Laura. E-mail interview. 8 May 2008. [When citing an interview you have conducted, indicate the type, such as personal interview, telephone interview, or e-mail interview.]

(Meng)

Meng, Dr. X. J. Interview. <u>Scientists</u>. Jan. 2008. 8 May 2008 <http://in-cites.com/scientists/XJMeng.html>. [When citing an interview conducted by someone else use the term interview.]

Lecture

(Roberts)

Roberts, Suzanne. Lecture. World History class. Cherry Creek High School, Greenwood Village, CO. 27 Apr. 2008.

Map

("Japan" 106)

"Japan." <u>Reader's Digest Atlas of the World</u>. Pleasantville: Reader's Digest Assn, 1990. 106–107.

(Konstam)

Konstam, Angus. "A Greek Dawn." <u>Historical Atlas of Ancient Greece</u>. New York: Mercury Books, 2003. 8–9.

("The Ancient World")

"The Ancient World, 600 BCE." <u>Maps 101: The Educational Resource Online</u>. 2008. Maps.com. 20 Apr. 2008 <http://www.maps101.com/>.

(<u>Wyoming</u>)

<u>Wyoming</u>. Map. Cheyenne: Wyoming Transportation Commission, 2001.

Media

(<u>To Kill</u>)

<u>To Kill a Mockingbird</u>. Dir. Robert Mulligan. Perf. Gregory Peck. 1962. DVD. Universal Studios, Apr. 28, 1998.

(<u>Energy</u>)

<u>Energy, Climate, and the Environment</u>. Perf. Denise Mauzerall. 8 Apr. 2008. You Tube. 23 Apr. 2008 <http://www.youtube.com/watch?v=i4GfUF-eVSc>.

Organization Website

("Germany")

"Germany." CountryReports.org. 27 Apr. 2008 <http://www. countryreports.org/>.

Personal Website

(Mullis)

Mullis, Kary. "The Benefits of Science." Kary Mullis. 2004 28 Apr. 2008 <http://www.karymullis.com/>.

Professional Website

(Archaeological Institute)

Archaeological Institute of America. 2008. Archaeological Institute of America. 23 Apr. 2008 <http://www. archaeological.org/>.

Sound Recording

(Ledbetter)

Ledbetter, Huddie. Leadbelly Sings Folk Songs. Perf. Leadbelly, Woody Guthrie, Cisco Houston, and Sonny Terry. Smithsonian Folkways Records, 1990.

(Judd)

Judd, Nathan. "The Answer to the Greenback Dollar." Voices from the Dust Bowl: The Charles L. Todd and Robert Sonkin Migrant Worker Collection, 1940–1941. 1940. American Memory. Lib. of Congress, Washington. 27 Apr. 2008 <http://memory.loc.gov/>.

Television or Radio Program

(Washington Week)

Washington Week. PBS. KRMA, Denver. 30 Apr. 2008.

("Supreme Court")

"Supreme Court Upholds Use of Lethal Injection." Washington Week. PBS. 18 Apr. 2008. Video 23 Apr. 2008 <http://www. pbs.org/weta/washingtonweek/video/index.html>.

ELECTRONIC CITATION TOOLS

There are a number of online tools available on the Internet that will help you format your citations. Your school may have a subscription to NoodleTools, Inc., or a link from your library website to Landmark's Citation Machine™. If you choose to use an online tool to assist you in preparing your citations and bibliography, be sure to double-check each citation against the style manual your instructor requires.

In addition, many electronic resources will provide citation examples for online resources. There are often discrepancies between these examples and specific style manuals. Consistency is critical in citing sources and the style manual required by your instructor is the primary guide to follow.

APPENDIX

APA SAMPLE CITATIONS

Sources used in research are documented in two ways. First, a parenthetical note acknowledges the source of information within the text of the paper. Second, a complete citation is listed on the final page of a research paper under the title "References". List the citations in alphabetical order and list only those sources actually used and cited in the paper.

For each type of source listed on the following pages, the parenthetical citation is shown first in parentheses as it would appear in the text. The full citation it refers to follows as it would appear in a references page.

This appendix has some of the most common types of references formatted in APA style. If you do not find an example that fits the source you are citing, refer to the *Publication Manual of the American Psychological Association*, the APA official website, or one of the online citation resources mentioned in Chapter 4. The important point to remember about citing sources is to be consistent. Remember, when in doubt, check with your librarian or instructor for guidance.

QUICK GUIDE TO CITATIONS

Number refers you to page where citation can be found.

Books

One Author

(Lynas, 2008, p. 281)

Lynas, M. (2008). *Six degrees: Our future on a hotter planet.* Washington, DC: National Geographic.

Two Authors

(Dow & Downing, 2006, p. 21)

Dow, K., & Downing, T. E. (2006). *The atlas of climate change.* Berkeley: University of California Press.

Three to Six Authors

(Hillman, Fawcett, & Sudhir, 2007, p. 24)

Hillman, M., Fawcett, T., & Sudhir, C. (2007). *The suicidal planet: How to prevent global climate catastrophe.* New York: St. Martin's.

No Author

(*American Heritage*, 2005, p. 268)

American Heritage science dictionary. (2005). Boston: Houghton Mifflin.

Editor

(Wood, 2004, p. 275).

Wood, R. A. (Ed.). (2004). *The weather almanac.* Detroit: Gale Research.

Corporate Author with Editor

(American Medical Association, 2006, p. 268)

American Medical Association (2006). *The American Medical Association concise encyclopedia of medicine.* (M. S. Lipsky, Ed.). New York: Random House.

Work in an Anthology

(Poe, 1845, p. 209)

Poe, E. A. (1845). The raven. In H. Felleman, *The best loved poems of the American people* (pp. 209–211). New York: Doubleday.

Multivolume Work with an Editor

(Considine, 2008, p. 2295)

Considine, G. D. (Ed.). (2008). *Van Nostrand's scientific encyclopedia* (Vols. 1–2). Hoboken, NJ: Wiley.

Multivolume Work with an Author and Editor

(Thurman, 1988, p. 182)

Thurman, R. A. F. (1988). Buddhism. In A. T. Embree (Ed.), *Encyclopedia of Asian history* (pp. 180–184). New York: Scribner's.

Multivolume Work with a Different Title for Each Volume

(Ecology, 2003, p. 57)

Ecology and environment: The cycles of life. (2003). In *The new encyclopedia of science* (Vol. 6). New York: Oxford University Press.

Excerpts from Criticism Cited in a Single Work

(Quinn, 1991, p. 430)

Quinn, A. H. (1991). Excerpts from Edgar Allan Poe: A critical biography. In R. V. Young (Ed.), *Poetry criticism* (Vol. 1, p. 430). Detroit: Gale Research.

Government Publication

(United States Census Bureau, 2006, p. 421)

United States Census Bureau. (2006). *Statistical abstract of the United States: 2007*. Washington, DC: U.S. Government Printing Office.

Almanac

(Some notable, 2007, p. 243)

Some notable new books, 2005. (2007). In *The world almanac and book of facts 2007* (p. 243). New York: World Almanac.

Pamphlet

(U.S. Department of Education, 2007, p. 9)

U.S. Department of Education. (2007). *Funding education beyond high school: The guide to federal student aid* [Pamphlet]. Washington, DC: U.S. Government Printing Office.

E-Book

(Johnson, 2002, p. 2)

Johnson, B. E. (2002). *The global warming desk reference* [Electronic version]. Westport, CT: Greenwood.

(Cooper, 2002, p. 121)

Cooper, J. F. (2002). *The deerslayer* [Electronic version. Etext-No.3285]. Project Gutenberg. Retrieved April 24, 2008, from http://www.gutenberg.org [When an electronic version of a book is believed to be an exact duplicate of the print version, it is not necessary to include the URL in the citation.]

Encyclopedias

Article from a General Encyclopedia with an Author

(Wertheim, 2004, p. 233)

Wertheim, A. (2004). Globe Theatre. In *The world book encyclopedia* (Vol. 8, pp. 233–234). Danbury, CT: Grolier.

Article from a General Encyclopedia without an Author

(Ballooning, 2001, p. 117)

Ballooning. (2001). In *Encyclopedia Americana* (Vol. 3, p. 117). Danbury, CT: Grolier.

Article from a Specialized Encyclopedia

(McKay, 2002, pp. 484)

McKay, A. (2002). Tibet. In D. Levinson & K. Christensen (Eds.), *Encyclopedia of modern Asia* (pp. 484–486). New York: Thomson.

Article from a General Online Encyclopedia

(Globe Theater, 2008)

Globe Theater. (2008). In *Wikipedia*. Retrieved April 24, 2008, from http://en.wikipedia.org/wiki

Article from a Specialized Online Encyclopedia

(Asian and near eastern art, 2008)

Asian and near eastern art. (2008). In *Encyclopedia Smithsonian*. Retrieved April 21, 2008, from http://www.si. edu/Encyclopedia_SI

Magazines

Article with an Author

(Gugliotta, 2008, p. 39)

Gugliotta, G. (2008, March). Rare breed. *Smithsonian*, 39, 38–47.

Article from a Subscription Database That Produces Its Own Information

(Clemmit, 2008, p. 290)

Clemmit, M. (2008, April 4). Preventing memory loss. *CQ Researcher*, 289–312. Retrieved April 27, 2008, from CQ Researcher database.

Article from a Subscription Database That Collects Information from a Variety of Sources

(Nash, 2007, p. 66)

Nash, M. J. (2007, July). Chronicling the ice. *Smithsonian*, 38, 66–74. Retrieved April 24, 2008, from MAS Ultra School Edition database.

Article from the Internet with an Author

(Gandel, 2008)

Gandel, C. (2008, March 21). Bamboo steps up. *Smithsonian.com*. Retrieved April 24, 2008, from http://www.smithsonianmag. com

Article from the Internet without an Author

(*Medical miracles*, 2008)

Medical miracles slipping away as extinction claims species (2008, April 23). Retrieved April 24, 2008, from Environment News Service database.

Newspapers

Article with an Author

(Pasternak, 2008, p. 7A)

Pasternak, J. (2008, April 24). EPA workers report political pressure. *The Denver Post*, p. 7A.

Article from a Subscription Database

(Fleming, 2008)

Fleming, S. (2008, April 12). UN issues alert over soaring food prices. *Daily Mail*. Retrieved April 24, 2008, from Newspaper Source database.

Article from an Online Newspaper

(Bodeen, 2008)

Bodeen, C. (2008, June 19). 100,000-strong force to protect Olympics. *The Washington Post*. Retrieved June 20, 2008, from http://www.washingtonpost.com

Editorial

(Cell phone, 2008, p. 30)

Cell phone rights. (2008, April 28). [Editorial]. *The Rocky Mountain News*, p. 30.

(Global warming, 2007)

Global warming and your wallet. (2007, July 6). [Editorial]. *The New York Times*. Retrieved April 29, 2008, from Newspaper Source database.

Specialized Sources

Art/Photographs

(Bierstadt, 1860)

Bierstadt, A. (Artist). (1860). *Rocky Pool, New Hampshire* [Oil on canvas]. Denver Art Museum, Denver, CO.

(da Vinci, c. 1503–1506)

da Vinci, L. (Artist). (c. 1503–1506). *Mona Lisa* [Oil on poplar]. Retrieved April 30, 2008, from http://louvre.fr/llv/ oeuvres/detail_notice.jsp

Article in Corporate Website

(*Learn*, 2008)

Learn about cancer. (2008). Retrieved April 22, 2008, from http://www.cancer.org/docroot/LRN/LRN_0.asp

Blog

(Anderson, 2008)

Anderson, B. (2008, April 28). *Arctic haze, a new culprit to warming.* Weblog entry posted to http://global-warming. accuweather.com

Cartoon

(White, 2008, p. A27)

White, G. (Cartoonist). (2008, April 28). *The New York Times*, p. A27.

(Toles, 2008)

Toles, T. (Cartoonist). (2008, April 28). *The Washington Post.* Retrieved April 30, 2008, from http://washingtonpost.com

Corporate Website

(*ESPN,* 2008)

ESPN: The world leader in sports. (2008). Retrieved April 23, 2008, from http://espn.go.com

E-mail Communication

(Anderson, 2008, April 30)

Personal communications including e-mail, letters, and personal interviews are not included in the reference list unless they have been published or posted online because they cannot be recovered. Cite this type of source only in the text of your paper. Only communication that can be recovered should be included in your reference list.

Interview

(Bush, 2008, May 8)

Personal communications including e-mail, letters, and personal interviews are not included in the reference list unless they have been published or posted online because they cannot be recovered. Cite this type of source only in the text of your paper. Only communication that can be recovered should be included in your reference list.

(Meng, 2008)

Meng, Dr. X. J. (Interviewee). (2008, January). *Scientists* [Interview]. Retrieved May 8 2008, from http://incites.com/ scientists

Lecture

(Roberts, 2008, April 27)

Personal communications including e-mail, letters, and personal interviews are not included in the reference list unless they have been published or posted online because they cannot be recovered. Cite this type of source only in the text of your paper. Only communication that can be recovered should be included in your reference list.

(Mauzerall, 2008)

Mauzerall, D. (Lecturer). (2008, April 8). Energy, climate, and the environment. Retrieved April 23, 2008, from http:// www.youtube.com/Watch?v=i4GfUF-eVSc

Map

(Japan, 1990, p. 106)

Japan. (1990). In *Reader's Digest atlas of the world.* Pleasantville, NY: Reader's Digest.

(Konstam, 2006)

Konstam, A. (2006). A Greek dawn. In *Historical atlas of ancient Greece* (pp. 8–9). London: Mercury Books.

(Ancient world, 2008)

The ancient world, 600 BCE. (2008). In *Maps 101: The educational resource online.* Retrieved April 20, 2008, from http://www.maps101.com database.

(*Wyoming*, 2001)

Wyoming [Map]. (2001). Cheyenne: Wyoming Transportation Commission.

Media

(Mulligan, 1962)

Mulligan, R. (Director). (1962). *To kill a mockingbird* [Digital video disc]. United States: Universal.

Organization Website

(*Germany*, 2008)

Germany. (2008). Retrieved April 27, 2008, from http://www. countryreports.org

Personal Website

(Mullis, 2004)

Mullis, K. (2004). *The benefits of science*. Retrieved April 28, 2008, from http://www.karymullis.com

Professional Website

(Archeological Institute, 2008)

Archeological Institute of America. (2008). Retrieved April 23, 2008, from http://www.archaeological.org

Sound Recording

(Ledbetter, 1990)

Ledbetter, H. (1990). Stewball [Recorded by Leadbelly]. On *Leadbelly sings folk songs* [CD]. New York: Smithsonian Folkways.

(Judd, 1940).

Judd, N. (1940). The answer to the greenback dollar. On *Voices from the dust bowl: The Charles L. Todd and Robert Sonkin migrant worker collection, 1940–1941*. Retrieved April 30, 2008, from http://memory.loc.gov

Television or Radio Program

(Supreme Court, 2008)

Supreme Court upholds lethal injection (2008, April 18). *Washington Week* [Television broadcast]. Denver: Public Broadcasting Service.

Television or Radio Program Online

(Supreme Court, 2008)

Supreme Court upholds use of lethal injection (2008, April 18). *Washington Week* [Television broadcast]. Retrieved April 23, 2008, from http://www.pbs.org/weta/washington week/video/index.html

SAMPLE PAPER

There is no specific requirement for the formatting of a title page for a research paper. What follows is an example only. Notice that the paper is double spaced throughout with indented first lines at the beginning of each new paragraph. The sample paper provides a possible example to follow, but always check with your instructor as to specific requirements for your assignment. These may include title page, spacing requirements, page numbering, and the "References" page. As you proofread your paper, always double-check any formatting requirements of your assignment.

Global Warming, Global Warning

Sara Castillo

Biology
Mr. Brooks
May 24, 2008

Global warming is causing a change in the earth's weather patterns that will have disastrous effects. ''Increasing human populations, rising affluence, and continued dependence on energy derived from fossil fuels are at the crux of the issue'' (Johnson, 2002, p. 2). Unless this issue is resolved and solutions are found, an environmental disaster will occur.

Scientists have studied past weather patterns and developed models to predict the future. According to Lynas (2008, p. 49) these models suggest we have not yet reached the critical tipping point, but it may not be far away. Scientists' expectations for climate change are supported by evidence gathered from around the world (Dow & Downing, 2006, pp. 20–21). The potential for major changes in the polar ice sheets in Greenland and Antarctica will cause an irreversible disaster (Hansen, 2007, p. 1). As our climate warms scientists warn that ''the depletion of resources on which livelihoods are based is the most critical effect of such change'' (Wagner, 2008, p. 1). Climate change will affect food production, water supplies, health, and ecosystems (Dow & Downing, 2006, pp. 54–61).

What is the cause of global warming? The use of fossil fuels for the past two centuries is generally accepted as the major cause of global warming (Johnson, 2002, p. 1). Lynas (2008, p. 281) concludes that we have only seven years before facing the danger of uncontrollable global warming. Nations struggle with reaching any universal agreement on how to reduce reliance on fossil fuels. In the meantime individuals can make a commitment to lifestyle changes to reduce the greenhouse gases emitted as a result of the way we live (Dow & Downing, 2006, p. 89).

REFERENCES

Dow, K., & Downing, T. E. (2006). *The atlas of climate change*. Berkeley: University of California Press.

Hansen, J. (2007). The world's most serious environmental problem is global warming [Electronic version]. In D. Miller (Ed.), *Current controversies: Pollution*. Westport, CT: Greenhaven, 2007. Retrieved April 24, 2008, from Opposing Viewpoints Resource Center database.

Johnson, B. E. (2002). *The global warming desk reference* [Electronic version]. Westport, CT: Greenwood.

Lynas, M. (2008). *Six degrees: Our future on a hotter planet*. Washington, DC: National Geographic.

Wagner, C. G. (2008, March–April). Climate change and global conflicts. *The Futurist, 42*, 6–7. Retrieved April 24, 2008, from WilsonSelect Plus database.

GLOSSARY

abridgment—A shortened version of the author's original work.

abstract—A summary or abridgment of the main points of a work, often written by someone other than the original author.

acknowledge—To give credit to another person's words, ideas, or opinions in the form of a note and/or bibliographic citation.

almanac—Annual publication containing information and statistics on major current and historical events.

analysis—A breaking up of a whole into its parts to examine them (often in a critical manner).

annotated bibliography—A bibliography with critical and/or explanatory notes about each source.

APA—American Psychological Association.

appendix—A section containing material not included in the body of a work but relevant to the topic.

authority—A generally accepted source of expert information.

autobiography—A person's life story written by himself or herself.

bibliography—A list of books, articles, and other material used in a work or compiled about a topic.

biography—An account of a person's life.

blog—Shortened form of "web log," which is a personal website with entries of opinions, descriptions of events, or other material such as graphics or video.

body (of a paper)—Refers to the paragraphs after the introduction and before the conclusion; contains the main points, ideas, and arguments of the author.

brackets—The punctuation marks [ ] used only within a quoted passage to enclose additions (which explain a work or give information to the reader) in the writer's own words; not the same as parentheses.

c. or ©—Copyright; date of publication usually follows.

c. or ca.—Circa, a Latin term meaning "about," used with approximate dates.

call number—The classification number located in the book's record on the online catalog screen and the book's lower spine. The two major classification systems are the Dewey Decimal System and the Library of Congress System.

CD-ROM—Compact Disc-Read Only Memory. Disc containing digital and/or graphic data read by a laser beam.

cite, citing, citation—Quote or quoting as an authority or example.

classify, classification—To arrange in classes or groups according to a system.

comp.—Compiled by, or compiler, a person who puts together a work composed of other individual works.

compare, contrast—To compare is to examine for similarities, to contrast is to examine for differences. Comparing and contrasting are often used together as a method of evaluation.

cross reference—Words or symbols that refer a reader to other places where additional information may be found.

descriptors—Keywords used in indexes; see keywords.

document—To acknowledge the source of an idea or fact with a parenthetical reference, end note, or footnote.

DVD—Digital video disc used for optical data storage.

ed. or eds.—Edited by; or editor(s), one who prepares something for publication by selecting and revising.

edition—The total number of copies of a work printed from a single set of type; each edition is printed at a different time and is given a distinct edition number.

editorial—An article expressing an opinion.

e.g.—For example, from the Latin exempli gratia; used to indicate that an example follows

ellipsis—Three periods with a space before, after, and between them (. . .) that indicate an omission in quoted material.

end notes—Documentation located at the end of a paper.

et al.—And others, from the Latin et alii; always abbreviated in bibliographic citations.

etc.—And so forth, from the Latin et cetera; avoid use.

footnote—Used to describe a citation placed at the bottom of a page. Parenthetical references and end notes are more commonly used.

general article—A relatively short article that gives a broad overview of a subject, usually located in encyclopedias or textbooks.

glossary—A dictionary section, usually at the end of a book, in which technical or difficult words are explained.

GPO—Government Printing Office, Washington, DC.

ibid.—In the same place, from the Latin ibidem; no longer recommended for use.

i.e.—That is, from the Latin id est.

intellectual property—Any creation of the mind such as musical, literary, or artistic works. The author or creator has exclusive rights to their own property and must be cited by anyone else using their work.

Internet service provider—A fee-based company that provides Internet access to individuals or businesses.

in-text documentation—See parenthetical reference.

keywords—Terms related to your topic, usually naming important places, people, and subject, that are used to search indexes and databases.

l., ll.—Line(s).

microform—Photographic reductions of pages of printed matter on film cards called microfiche or on rolls of film called microfilm.

MLA—Modern Language Association.

monograph—A book complete in one volume.

ms., mss.—Manuscript, manuscripts.

n.d.—No date of publication given.

n.p.—No publisher given; no place of publication given.

n. pag.—No paging given in source.

online database—Computer access to databases of holdings of academic and public libraries, specialized indexes, and information services.

outline—A general plan of a work; an organizational tool that encourages the writer to determine the main points of the presentation and the divisions under those points; can take a number of forms including topic, sentence, phrase, word, and preliminary.

p., pp.—Page, pages.

paraphrase—To put another's idea, opinion, or argument into one's own words.

parentheses—The punctuation marks ( ) used to enclose your own explanatory materials in a phrase or sentence of your own; use sparingly.

parenthetical reference—Documentation located within the text of a research paper; currently the favored method for most research papers.

peer review—Process of submitting an author's work to criticism and evaluation by others.

periodicals—Publications, such as magazines, journals, or newspapers, that are published at regular intervals.

plagiarism—Using another's style, ideas, or phrasing without giving credit.

podcast—Content that may be downloaded or streamed but may also be subscribed to and downloaded automatically when there is new content.

preliminary bibliography—(Sometimes called a working bibliography) a list of sources containing the needed information about materials available on a topic; used to see the scope of sources and to help narrow the thesis.

primary source—Work, manuscript, journal, government document as originally written. Some examples of primary sources are a diary, letter, legislative bill, interview, poem, experiment, autobiography, and survey.

prod.—Produced by, producer.

pseudonym—Fictitious name used by an author.

reference book—Any source designed to be consulted for information rather than to be read in its entirety.

Roman numerals—Numbering system used in outlines, for preliminary pages in books, and sometimes in volume numbers (I = 1, II = 2, III = 3, IV = 4, V = 5, VI = 6, VII = 7, VIII = 8, IX = 9, X = 10, L = 50, C = 100).

rough draft—The first and any other writing before the paper is put into final form; rough drafts often require several revisions.

rpt.—Reprint, reprinted by.

secondary source—A critical or historical work based on the primary source such as textbooks, encyclopedias, or biographies.

series—Thematically connected multivolume works.

subject headings—Subjects assigned to a particular book, highlighted in the online catalog bibliographic record.

thesis—The statement that explains the opinion or idea the writer wishes to support.

tr., tran.—Translator, translation, or translated by.

vol., vols.—Volume(s), numbers may be written in Arabic Roman numerals.

works in progress—Works continued with volumes published at intervals; usually have cumulative indexes.

BIBLIOGRAPHY

American Psychological Association. *Publication Manual of the American Psychological Association.* 5th ed. Washington: American Psychological Association, 2001.

Gibaldi, Joseph. *MLA Handbook for Writers of Research Papers.* 6th ed. New York: Modern Language Association, 2003.

Lester, James D., Sr., and James D. Lester, Jr. *The Research Paper Handbook.* Glenview: Good Year Books, 1992.

Markman, Roberta H., Peter T. Markman, and Marie L. Waddell. *10 Steps in Writing the Research Paper.* Hauppauge: Barron's, 1994.

Index

ABOUT THE AUTHORS

ELIZABETH BANKHEAD is a longtime practitioner and advocate for "teaching libraries" with over 30 years of experience as a school library media specialist at all levels. She has developed nationally recognized library programs including being selected as a recipient of the "National School Library Media Program of the Year" Award. Betty is an active member of the American Association of School Librarians (AASL) and is the author and presenter of the first AASL Leadership Institute, "Collaborative Leadership." Betty has also served for the past seven years as the director of staff development for the Colorado Power Libraries.

JANET NICHOLS is the former coordinator of instruction and information services at the David Adamany Undergraduate Library, Wayne State University, Detroit, Michigan. Prior to working in higher education, she spent 25 years in K–12 education as an English teacher, reading specialist, and school librarian.

DAWN VAUGHN has been a school library media specialist for more than 25 years. She has worked at all levels of libraries in three states and is passionate about the teaching and leadership role of the library media specialist in schools. An active member of the American Association of School Librarians, she served as president from 2004 to 2005. Dawn is experienced in professional development, presenting at conferences and workshops at the local, state, and national levels throughout her career. Most recently, she has been an administrator at a large suburban high school.